AF398399

Language proofreading of Christine Mathiesen

Foreword

About me, I was born in east/south Norway in 1950. Since 2020 I have lived in unity with my soul/higher self and travel all around the world and perform my life callings.

To follow any religions or tradisjon have never come into my mind.

Since birth I have been in contact with other realities and dimensions.

Talking with angels I hav done all my life, and started channelings with my angel friends and other masters in 2018 and we have together created 5 books.

For me it was important to let them deside the books titels and cover.

Welcome to my magical world, where I have conversations with my higher self/soul, archangel Seraphim. He is the guardian angel of the Muslims, just as Christianity has archangel Michael.

And my life mission soul Osiris, who sends me on journeys across the earth to cleanse negative energy and help the dead home after the wars.
And to introduce the unity back into nature, while creating lines around the earth, to keep the earth in its oval journey in our universe around our star the sun.
Osiris also takes me traveling with my consciousness into the different universes.

(Osiris was the Egyptian god who landed in the desert of Egypt in a UFO from the planet Sirius, and he says it was about 8000 years ago.)

Everything in the book is conversations recorded on
my phone.
I choose to use regular font for my words, and I use
bold for the words of my souls and the Elements.

The conversations are directly transferred to the book
as my souls ask me to, so you may be able to sense
their energy.
Sometimes they say us, we and you.

Experience

Journey through the heart of Osiris into another reality!

A big explosion is shown to me.
What is it Osiris, is it "The Big Bang" I see?

That's it, dear.
Now we're going to travel into another reality, Illia, that you haven't been to before, but don't be afraid because there's nothing dangerous there.
It's just beautiful there, Illia.

Thank you, Osiris.
I see we are approaching a fog. A pink, foggy mass.

It's just as if I'm melting in my body. Just as if my body is falling into place, into a new place.

Here the reality is pure love, Illia, nothing but pure.

Am I becoming one with the Divine light of love I have seen?

You are in it now, Illia.

There are many here, so magical!
So strange, just as if everyone is in their own little
love cell.
And the love here is so strong, it transforms my body,
Osiris.

Say hello to everyone around you, Illia, you will
recognize them.

Do I, Osiris?
No, this is Seraphim speaking now.

You will recognize them, Illia, they are your sisters
and brothers in other realities.

Oh, there I see Araka the elf queen.
Hello dear friend, dear sister.

I have been waiting for you to come here and become
one with me.
I am just another part of you.

Are you, Araka?

You are our great goddess, Illia, you are the archangel
Seraphim, you know. The greatest of them all, and we
are one with you.

I can't quite understand it, Araka.

I can understand that, Illia, it's many-faceted you see.
There is a many-faceted reality here with us, but we
are all separate beings.

Who is in the next bubble, is it you, Fria?
Angel of the air, are you under Seraphim?

All the elements are under Seraphim, Illia.

Oh, I see you, Fria, angel of the air, your beautiful
long, flowing hair. How beautiful.

Razul angel of the earth, is there too.
Oh God, how strong this is, Osiris.

I know, Illia, you needed this, you see, to get higher.

Hello Razul and hello Ea, and the moon goddess
Serafa, too.
Is there anyone else you want me to see?

That's enough for now.

Thank you, dear Osiris, thank you dear Seraphim.
So strong, I feel shaken and filled with love deep in
my heart now.

**We can understand that dear Illia, it is important
that you understand how important you are, you see.
You hold the entire nearest universe together Illia, as
you are the archangel Seraphim.**

(When we are born in a feminine body, our higher
self/soul is usually masculine, unless you have chosen
to experience the imbalance by being gay or lesbian,
or other forms of gender. And it's the opposite with a
masculine body, feminine angel. Yin and yang in the
same being.)

ANGELS of the ELEMENTS

29-8-21

I am now beginning the channeling of the book "ANGELS of the ELEMENTS" where I channel the spiritual beings/angels of all the elements:

Earth – Razul

Water – Ea

Air – Fria

Fire – Arakto

Razul

Angel of the Earth

I am told by my higher self/soul archangel Seraphim that I should start the book with the angel of the Earth.

I have always thought of the angel of the earth as feminine, Yaya, and then I call her by saying out loud, dear Yaya!

Suddenly I feel a strong force, and right in front of me stands a large masculine angel. He says in a loud voice:

My name is Razul!

I jumped at the power of his voice, which was incredibly strong.

Greetings angel of the earth, Razul, what would you like to share with us about your being?

I want to share with you the being of my consciousness, and being a caretaker, the one who

takes care of earth as a planet and consciousness in its position in the universe.

That sounds exciting, Razul.

I want to say that existence is something that moves us deeply. To be a being in the whole, in the totality of the universe is a magical experience.

How do you feel that experience, Razul, what can you tell us about it?

I feel it as a flow of love and excitement, in my consciousness.
Being one with everything, but still being the earth.

I had to stop after a short channeling, it was such a powerful transformation when Razul used my voice, so I only managed three minutes!

30-8-21
Razul says I'm open now, so I'm really channeling well. And when he speaks with my voice, it's like I hear his voice in my whole body, in all my cells.

The other angels I hear in my heart, but I hear his voice in my whole body! He fills the whole room I'm sitting in and the whole area around me with his powerful energy.

I am the greatest on earth, you know. I am the consciousness of the element earth. Like a big conscious ball I float in the universe.
And it's a magic ball, a magical planet, which is made up of many consciousnesses in its being.

Everything is unity, as you experience that everything is GOD.

It becomes very strong when you use my voice, Razul, it moves my whole body.

Yes, you are a strong master, Illia.

Thank you, I can't quite feel it, Razul, but I'm working on feeling valuable, feeling good enough. But there are still remnants of my limitations and inferiority.

Take part of my energy, Illia, and it will disappear.

Now my back twitched really hard and uncomfortably. I have never been pulled so hard in early healings during a channeling.

This is strong stuff, Illia. My element is a being in motion, it's continuous movement like all other energy and consciousness is perpetual movement towards something new.

People are so worried that so many races are disappearing from earth, but new races are coming which have not been seen before.
Because there are new changes coming to earth and it's also coming into your bodies. Your bodies are also renewed together with nature, but you need to stop the pollution.
You can't go on with it any longer, you know. Do as Illia and buy everything from the health store, shampoo and soaps for your body and house.
It's important, because there you pollute a lot, into the water and into earth's consciousness.
And the air is important, so drive a car as little as possible and take the bus.
Public transport is designed to save the environment, so use your legs and bicycles.

I hope people can wake up and become more aware,
and take care of not only their house, but everything
around them as a whole.

Yes, Illia, everything is connected as a whole.

Not many people realize this, Razul.

**And we are very sorry about it, Illia. But it will
happen now, you see. When you send love out to earth
all the time, people will wake up more and more, Illia.
Because you are the greatest master on earth now.
You know it, you know you are, but you can't take it
in.**

I can't, but I hear you say it. My soul says it but being
able to take it in and integrate it, Razul, is something
completely different.
But this book is not about me.

**Yes, it is, Illia, this book is about you and your
cooperation with the elements.**

You talk to all the elements, Illia, so it's your life together with the elements that we're going to talk about in this book.

Okay, is there anything else you want to tell us today?

Much more, Illia, much more.
Now you let go of control a little more, Illia. You needed that, you see, because you still have a great fear of authority and of the spiritual that is still stuck in you. It's on its way out, but it will take some time, you see, before it disappears completely.

(From my first book "Bullied into love", where they tell me that they had to scare me away from my spiritual life as a two-year old, because I only wanted to die and disappear into my paradise dimension. The masters had to scare me in order to survive and fulfil my life mission.)

Thank you. What would you like to continue the conversation with, Razul?

The element earth is a magical element like the other elements, Illia. It is a substance on a completely different level from the other elements, just as they are also a completely different substance from our other elements.

I notice that you are not used to speaking physically Razul, because you struggle to use my voice and speak through me.

Yes, this is my first time channeling a human.

Thank you, Razul, for trusting me. Thank you!

It is I who should thank you, Illia, for being heard.

This is so strong, Razul, I'm starting to cry a lot.

Yes, you feel my grief, Illia, of not being heard by the people who are destroying my earth.

Oh, Razul, but this is getting so strong for me, I really must stop.

I understand that, Illia, but we will see each other again soon. We'll meet at our next call, but I'm with you all the time.

Are you, Razul?

I am, Illia, I'm with you all the time. We have been together for a long time now, all the elements are with you all the time, Illia. You are one with us, you see, on a very high level. Actually, you're the only one on earth who talks to us elements.

I feel your healing, it burns inside my whole body now, Razul.

I am burning away old limitations, Illia. You need to let go of all old limitations, dear master Illia.

I must stop now, I can't take it anymore, so powerful!

I understand, we have been talking for nine minutes. That's good, thank you.

Thank you, Razul, I feel so moved in my whole body!

21-11-21

As you can see, my channelings are few and far between! It is powerful stuff, and I'm still running away from my spiritual life a lot.

Now I am back on La Gomera, Spain, and today Razul will channel more about his element.

Dear angel of the Earth Razul, what would you like to share with us about your being?

Gomera is a strong place, anything can happen here.

I live here in the mountains and count on you to be with me.

We are, dear.

How will you continue about your element earth today, Razul?

I will begin by telling you, Illia, that you are a very important medium for us elements.

I feel the love you give me in my heart, Razul, when you say that.

You are a very important medium to communicate to the humans who we really are.
Why we really are here, for the good of humanity.
So that they can connect with us on many levels and realities.

That sounds great, Razul. What do you want to start with, Razul?
You want to start with the story of creation?

Yes, I would like to.
Creation began with the words of God, LET IT BE!
Then particles began to gather.

How did it come together as a physical planet in relation to other planets?

All planets are physical, but you live in the physical reality of earth. On other planets they live in other realities which exist specifically for their planet.

So all planets have different realities?

All planets have the same realities as earth, but it is only here on earth that you live in the physical reality.

Okay, so it's only on planet earth that we live in the physical reality out of all the planets?

Yes, on all other planets they live in different realities which we don't have contact with here on earth.
You have it, Illia, but there are very few people who have contact with all realities on earth.

So you want to talk about the realities that exist here on earth?

Yes, I would love to.
There are many realities on earth. The first one is the physical one, and then comes the emotional reality, which everyone knows from feelings.

It's the first layer of your aura, and the first layer of the earth's aura.

So that's the emotional layer we humans live in?

It is.

What's the next level?

The next level is the thoughts' reality, which is further away from the physical. It's the next layer of consciousness.

So, beyond that then, Razul, what lies beyond thought reality?

**There lies the etheric reality.
The etheric reality also has its dimensions.**

What do you mean by that, Razul?
Different realities also have their different dimensions of realities, is that what you mean?
So many realities in each dimension? The thought dimension has many different realities?

That's how it is.

Wow, so strong to hear that.

We know, not many people have heard about this, you know.

They keep talking, Razul, about there being life inside the earth.

Yes, there is, Illia, but we haven't gotten there yet. We're staying on the surface now; we'll get there eventually during the day.

It will be strong, Razul.

It will be a new revelation for you all to understand the realities here on earth.

It's very exciting, Razul, I'm looking forward to it.

Now we're going to start with the inner thought reality.

What do you mean by that, Razul, the origin of thought creation?

Here's how it is.

We create with our thoughts, but we don't know
where the creative energy comes from.

Okay, that's what you meant. What else do you want
to tell us about the dimensions on earth?

Earth is a place where all dimensions meet in
different realities.
We have the thought dimension, the feeling reality
and the ethereal spiritual realities.

There they are divided by different realities in the
different dimensions.

Does it have to do with the element earth, Razul?

It's important to know what earth is like, on all levels.

Getting very strong healing from you, Razul!

My healing is strong, Illia, you need it, you
understand. To fully connect with mother earth, you
need my energy and healing.

I would like to tell you about the limitations we face
here on earth in this dimension of physical being.
The physical being here on earth is very limited, but
we can choose to be in the heavenly being on earth.
It is entirely up to everyone what we want to focus
on.
You have been told that by your souls, haven't you?

I certainly have, Razul.

We have to choose, everything is always a choice.
Are you going to choose to be in the primitive part of
mother earth, are you going to choose to be in the
mother earth of emotion and pain?
Or will you choose to be in the mother earth of love?
Then you will encounter many realities on a
completely different level than the physical.

Oh, so strong, I think I will write this down first. Then
we'll move on to each dimension in turn?

It's okay, dear, because you get very strong healing
from me.

Very strong, Razul, my whole body is shaking.

Thank you for now, Razul.

26-11-21

I began to talk about dimensions and realities on earth, and now I will continue.

There are many realities on earth that humans do not experience, which you have experienced much of Illia. But still there is more you haven't experienced, Illia.

Is it, Razul?

Oh, yes Illia, there are many dimensions on earth, many realities.

I will start with the emotional reality, which is closest to the physical crust.

Emotional reality is the concept of emotions, as we know, pain is also in the emotional body, along with emotions.

There are also many realities there.

Which realities are they, Razul?

Realities of beings that help you experience pain.
Helping you to feel what you are about to learn, of
pain and emotion.

You mean the ones that are placed in our aura, which
we must experience in order to become who we're
supposed to become.
And experience what we're supposed to experience?

That's right, dear.

Okay, that's where they are.

There are so many layers upon layers that create us
to become who we are to be in this life.
We think we have created ourselves, that we are an
independent being.
But we are just empty shells when we not are being in
oneness with the soul.
Then we are given thoughts and beliefs in our aura,
which will give us qualities and personality.

Yes, I think I have cleansed hundreds, Razul.

Yes, you probably have, Illia, there are not so many left with you now.

Not really, I've been cleaning it out for a very long time now.
It was February 2020 when I learned how many dead souls have been laid upon us in our aura.

I want to ask about something, Razul, are there also different things that can trigger us in that feeling reality?

Absolutely, Illia, there are many different beings there.

So that's where they are, in our feeling energy field.

It certainly is, Illia.

Are you done talking about the emotional plane?

I am, Illia.

What's next, Razul, the thought aura/energy field?

It will be, and in the thought aura it's also the same style.
The same energy beings that hang on and give you thoughts that you will experience, to become who you will be in this life.

There are also those who will keep us away from the light, right Razul?

A lot of beings will keep you away from the path of light, because they feed on fear here on earth.

That's why it's important to be highly observant of your thoughts. Finding out which thoughts are yours is very important.

Yes. Is there anything else in the thought reality, Razul?

There are many dimensions to the thought reality as well, Illia. But the most important thing to do with thoughts is hearing and listening, and finding out which are your own truths, and which come from your aura.
That is very important.

Is there anything else there, Razul, that you want us to know?

Yes, there is also a layer there of history that can be listened to and received.
That's why it's important to know your own thoughts.
What is history and what exists in the here and now, your own story.

Are there any other realities there, Razul?

No, these are the three realities: your thoughts, other people's thoughts and historical thoughts.
It's so important to know what you think, what thoughts you have with you from birth, which are yours and not someone else's that come into your aura.

What's the next layer there then, Razul, is it the etheric layer?

It's the ethereal spiritual layer, Illia, and here we also have many dimensions, you see.

Okay, I'm very excited to hear about that, Razul!

Yes, look forward to it, Illia.
Here in the first layer, there are goblins and elves.

So that is the first layer of the ethereal, okay.
I'm thinking of the first layer, with goblins and elves.
Are they there to be with us and help us?
And how can we interact with goblins and elves,
Razul?

I just want you to know that they are there for you.
They are there to support you and help you on many
levels, much more than you think.
You Illia have met both elves and gnomes several
times, so you know they exist.
You have experienced it so clearly without having
looked for them, but they have come and shown
themselves to you, Illia.

Absolutely, many magical moments.

Angels are the next layer, Illia.

Yes, I have seen many angels in different shapes, colours, and realities, I was about to say.
Some are very, very big and fill large halls, while others are more normal sized.
They can also be smaller. Angels I have seen from other planets are smaller.

But there are angels on another reality, Illia, like Osiris' angel Ammari. She is quite small and blue but larger than ordinary humans.

Yes, she is.
This is very exciting, Razul. So the angels are in the earth's sphere, the earth's ethereal reality?

They are, Illia, everything exists in the earth's spheres.

Is there more outside there, what's outside there, aliens?

No, the aliens belong to other planets, and they come to visit.
The third sphere contain the spheres of light beings.

Are they outside the angels?

That's it dear, the balls of light you see are dead
people who are still in the earth sphere.
Because they don't want to move on, or they are here
to help you.

So those balls of light called orbs, are they dead
people?

They could be, but they could also be from other
planets coming here.
Or from the other side coming to help you.

What's the next layer then, Razul?

Then there are no more layers there, Illia. There will
be layers inward, within the earth's crust.

Yes, many people wonder about that, Razul!

We know that, Illia, you have heard that there is life
inside earth, and it is true. But not physical life, Illia.

No, I didn't expect that either, Razul, inside the red-
hot earth.

There are other realities, it's not only a red-hot reality inside of earth.
It's not just liquid lava in there, there are also other realities inside.
And one reality, Illia, is an angelic reality which is inside the earth, you see.

Is there an angelic reality inside the earth?

Yes, but humans have believed there are ordinary people inside earth, but it doesn't exist in there.
There is an angelic reality in there, earthly angels living inside the earth's energy field.

Wow, are there more layers there?

You have the trolls, Illia, whom you love so much and with whom you have contact.

Yes, they're so lovely.
I'll never forget the troll who came to visit me when I was on the train from Bergen.

It ran! A big pile of stones running next to the train and speaking to me!
He said: I've heard about you!

(That was because I was talking to two trolls on the train on the way to Bergen.
I couldn't quite believe them, and thought they were dead souls on the train talking to me.
But when he came running! Well, then I just had to realize they exist.)
It was a totally surreal experience, Razul.

Yeah, but they're our friends, you know.

Yes, but there are so many sad and scary stories written about trolls, so sad.

Yeah, they'll do anything to scare you away from the natural, you know.

Yes, I know, Razul.
Is there anything else you want to tell me about the spheres of earth, Razul?

No, that's enough for today, Illia. That's enough for today.

Is there more than that, Razul?

Much more, Illia, on a whole different level than you know.

How exciting.
Do I feel, do I sense dragons within the earth?

There are dragons in the earth, Illia.

Is it, Razul?

It really is, along with the angels. But in a slightly different reality/dimension than the angels, the dragons are, Illia.

29-11-21
We got as far as what lives inside the earth last time, Razul. Would you like to say something more about that perhaps?

Much more.
I want to tell you about the dimensions inside earth,
where consciousnesses live. Not physical, but other
realities.

My whole lower body is twitching, Razul.

I am healing your root chakra, Illia.
Today I will start with the first layer after the lava.
The first layer of solid mass.

What kind of beings live there, and in what reality do
they live in?

They live in a sphere of oneness with the All, with
mountains, lava, and everything in the mineral
kingdom.

Do they have any form of their own?

They have a form of their own, dear, but it's not so
obvious. Like you saw on Sirius with Osiris.
They float like a body but without legs and hands. But
with a body with a head on top.

Like a mineral mass, not liquid but ethereal, mineral mass.

(I was on a consciousness journey with Osiris, my life's mission soul, to the planet/star Sirius.
There they floated in an ethereal blue mass. And everyone was blue, even the angels. From the book "Planets and Realities".)

What are they doing there, do they have a mission to be there?

Their mission is to make sure lava doesn't flow when it's not supposed to, Illia.

Do people who live inside there have a name?

They're Sorotians.

Sorotians!
Exciting, Razul. What's the next layer?

**The next layer is a void.
A cavity between this layer and the next layer.
A cavity where they live as elves, trolls, and goblins.**

Elves, goblins and trolls live inside the earth too?

It's on a different level than those who live on the earth's surface, Illia.

Maybe I should have thought about that, since those on earth are visible to those who see and believe in something more.

That's so, dear.

What kind of life do they have, do they have a body?

They have a body on a spiritual level, like angels have bodies, dear.

In a way they are angelic beings inside the earth, as elves, gnomes and trolls?

They are dear, but less physical, more ethereal form. They live in a different layer, like it's above earth and inside earth as well.
The ethereal is there, they have their own bodies but still they are in the spiritual angelic world.

So is there a special name for them?

No, they have the same ones as above ground, elves, gnomes, and trolls.

Then they're more ethereal in form than the ones I've met.

That's so.

Okay, now I'm really excited about the next level.

I can understand that, Illia, the next level is magical, you know. It's almost physical, Illia.

Is it?

Yes, it's a cross between what you're experiencing here and the fairy realm.

Could it be almost physical in there?

It can, Illia, but it's physical on a different level than what we're physically used to.

What do you mean, Razul?

They live in a mass, like a holistic mass.
In a way that you were shown that everyone has their
own little bubble.
You can see their essence, yet they have no form of
their own.

Okay, like cells that I saw in the Divine Love Light?

It's like that.

But how do they work if they are just a cellular form
in the Oneness? Is that so, dear?

That's how it is. It's more physical than in the angelic
realm, yet they have less form.

What do you call them, then?

Beings in physical essence.

So they are beings in physical essence, not manifested
physically you mean?

That's how it is.

Was that the last layer before the crust?

It is, dear, and there are others.
Also, angels who hold the earth together work on one level to hold the earth together.

Now they are working hard between La Gomera, El Hierro and La Palma to create new land, Illia.

It has been shown that there will be new land and a large island in the end.

Illia, it will be, but it will take many years.

Thank you, Razul. Have you finished channeling the element of earth?

I am, Illia.

Thank you, Razul.
Oh, you're the one who wants to thank me?

You are the first to listen to me, Illia!

Oh God, your healing is so strong, Razul.
I feel it very much in the hara and root chakras!

I am healing you now, Illia.

I can feel it, Razul. Thank you very much.

Is Ea coming as the next element, Razul?

She is, good luck with Ea.

Thank you dear Razul.

To Razul

I met you Razul angel of the earth.
I was startled, because I was sure
the earth was feminine.

But there you stood before me angel Razul
and told me clearly with your energy.

You are not feminine,
you are pure masculine power,
not feminine.
Thank you for embracing me wherever I go.

Thank you!

Ea

The angel of water

My first meeting with Ea was when I moved to
Kråkerøy in 2001. I heard about Smertudammen, a
beautiful little pond filled with water lilies, near to
where I live.
One evening when I'm sitting looking down and
greeting Smertudammen, I see a dancing angel
floating over the water towards me.
Such a magical and beautiful experience, Ea.
I recognize the mood from the experience when I
write about this our first meeting, dear.

Another experience with water was when I was on
the plane home from La Gomera a year ago.
I asked Seraphim if I could do something, sitting at
the window seat on the plane.

Seraphim said:
**Send love and become one with the clouds, and love
will rain down all over earth.**

But Seraphim, I only fly over a small part of the Atlantic Ocean.

You remember, Illia, that Ea/water has memory. So when you send love to the clouds, your great power of love spreads into all water on earth, and into people's bodies as well.

29-11-21
My first conversation with Ea

Dear Ea goddess of water, do you also have different realities and dimensions like Razul?

Of course I do, Illia.

How exciting, I look forward to hearing your story about your realities and dimensions, Ea.

I am first and foremost water, in all levels in all places.

Do you have different realities in your water?

There are many realities in water, one type of water
is inside your bodies.
In your blood and in all your muscles and tissues.

I feel you in my whole body now, I feel you touching
all the water in my body.

I am moving your water now dear, so you get to
experience me on a different level than you are used
to.

Actually, I've been a bit worried about swimming in
you, Ea. I was so weak after I was sick, before I
started channeling the books. That's why I haven't
been able to fight the waves.
So I have been close to drowning twice. Especially in
Crete two years ago. If that couple hadn't come by on
the beach just then I would have drowned.
And that made me afraid of your power, dear Ea.
I didn't have the contact with you that I have now.

I was with you, I had looked after you, you see.
Seraphim is my master, Illia.

Is he?

Seraphim is the leader of all the elements, Illia, here on earth. As long as he is on earth with you, he is the leader of all elements and all angels.

That was powerful to hear, I'm shaking all over my body now.

Oh, I feel it shaking all over me, Ea.

Now I'm in your bloodstream, Illia.

Wow, I can feel you flowing through me.

We are so grateful that you know about us and talk to us, dear.

Yes, Seraphim has told me.
He said that I'm the first human here on earth talking to you.
Like person to person, I mean person to angel.

We are very grateful for that, Illia.

I must say I find it very powerful to be able to talk to you. I didn't know it was possible until I started talking to Vileda.
It was she who opened me up to the elements, Ea.
(Vileda is the angel of the sun.)

We know all about that, she told us, now today we can do it!

She did?

Yes, she did.

Oh, how beautiful.
It was in the mountains of Soria in Fernando's "jardin magico airb&b" in Gran Canaria, Spain.

That was it dear, and after that it has been a magical journey with you, dear.

Has it? So nice to hear. I am really moved when you say that, because I feel you touch all the water in me, dear.
A very powerful and beautiful experience.

When I look at water now, Ea, I see a big body.
It's a bit strange to think about, but you must be a
very big angel.

I'm not such a big angel, Illia, but I'm in all water.
My consciousness is in all water.
Even though I have my own angelic body, my
consciousness is in all water.

I understand, dear one, that you are in all water.
When I saw you, you were the size of an ordinary
angel filling a ballroom.

I am in consciousness as Araka.
Araka, the elf queen, is in all plants on earth.
Then she has her favourite plant she has taken up
residence in, in this life here.
She chose the climbing hydrangea.

Which dimension of your water have you chosen to be
in this life, dear Ea?

I have chosen to be in the ocean, Illia.

So then I see your body of consciousness as all water
at once!

You do, dear, the totality of my consciousness.

The ocean needs our energy now.

Yes, it certainly does, with all the pollution we're
doing.

**Yeah, you're good at that, when you're not in your
heart, you know.**

It's so sad.

Don't get upset Illia, they're no wiser, you see.

No, I know, dear.

**They're not ready to go that way yet you see. Some
are, but not so many, dear.**

I wish everyone was and cared about doing something
for the earth.
Imagine how nice we could all exist together.

I get it, Illia, but it's not like that.
It is not time yet, but it's coming very fast, you see.

Yes, it's happening very fast now.

Very fast Illia, much faster than you think, you see.

That's good, I've been so worried.

Your worries are over now, my dear.

So I'm not supposed to worry about the earth anymore?

By all means, you know this, Illia. The more you worry, the more you get to worry about the earth! Stop worrying now, instead know that everything is fine.

Thank you dear, it sounds good.
I choose to believe that I can do it, dear.

You'll feel so much better when you let go of all worries, dear.

That's good, I'm glad to hear it, Ea.

That was a dimension of you, Ea, being in the oceans.
What do you want to tell me next?

I'd like to start with the ethereal water, Illia.

What is meant by ethereal water?

**Ethereal water, Illia, is at a completely different level
than you know what water is.
Essential water is a being in the water, in the oceans.**

You mean those who live in the sea?

No, water itself.

So how will I experience ethereal water?

It is a mass of love, Illia, a mass of love.

It sounds exciting, is it a shape, a colour?
Can we see it as something?

See it as a being, the being of consciousness in all water.

You mean the consciousness of water? I thought it was you, Ea. I don't quite understand.

It doesn't matter, dear, you will understand anyway, you see.

Thank you, dear, it's good to hear that I do.

You certainly do, dear, you are with us all the time, Illia.

I'm glad you still think so. I don't feel like I've been with you so much lately.

You're with us much more than you realize, Illia.

So it's the consciousness in water itself that is the etheric water, which is then a dimension in water. Is it the memory in water you're thinking of, dear?

It is, dear, water has memory, you've heard that.

Yes, very exciting.

So all water remembers everything that has happened to it.

Now I feel currents of energy from water right into my body here I am sitting by the sea and talking to you, Ea.

It's dancing for you now, Illia.

Yes, I can feel it, I can feel it dancing in my whole body, my dear. Here I sit and watch the beautiful waves washing over the sand.
It was the consciousness in the water, which is not you but still you.

It is me on another level, Illia.

Now I understand, Ea.

Oh, there I see you, Ea, a big angel dancing over the water in front of me.
Oh God, how beautiful you are, I start to cry because it's such a powerful experience dear Ea.

I am so grateful that you exist. I love watching and listening to water, water is so magical.

You are touching me very strongly now Ea.

You have reached a very special level now Illia.

What level is that, Ea?

It is the awareness of being within being.

I didn't understand that, Ea?

Well, you are aware that you exist, so the consciousness of water in being is also aware that it is a being as a whole.

Isn't that you then, Ea?

A part of me.

That's powerful, Ea.
So water is aware that it is present and that it is water, do you mean?

The water is aware of its existence in the All.

In our bodies and in all ponds, lakes, and oceans?

Yes, Illia.

Can you please explain in another way that everything
is consciousness?

This is consciousness within consciousness, Illia.

Consciousness in the consciousness that there is water,
and it exists everywhere?

That's how it is, dear.

Okay, that's so powerful.
Is there more about water you want to tell me, Ea?
Are there more dimensions you want to tell me
about?

I just want to tell you, Illia, water loves mother earth.
Water loves to touch your bodies.
Water loves to be in you, Illia, in the divine love of
everything in everything.

Oh, so strong, Ea.

With sound, water is trying to create better feelings
for you all the time.
Better versions of what you were thinking and feeling,
all the time.
Mirror yourself in the surface of water, and the ocean
reflects something good back which is beautiful,
thoughtful and loving.

Thank you, dear.
Are you done, Ea?
You really touched me now, Ea. Very much so in a
special way.

I talked to big brother Jesus earlier and he said I
didn't have to be afraid of drowning!
He said my souls would carry me and that you would
make your body/water solid for my sake.

I would like to make my body firm for your sake dear,
so you can step on me. I would like that.

I'm glad to hear, very glad to hear that dear Ea.

Very beautiful, thank you for our magical conversation, Ea.

Thank you, dear, who will listen to me.

I would like to listen a lot, dear.

2-12-21
Dear Ea, I really wonder about the fact that each drop of water is also a being, or consciousness. Isn't that right, Ea?

It certainly is, Illia, there is consciousness within the consciousness that we have just channeled, dear ones. There are divine light cells in all that is, so all water drops are also love-light cells.

So that's the love-light consciousness which is in all water, in all water drops.
Like Leo, who helped me write the first book, told me to play with the soap bubbles in the dishes!

That's how it is, Illia, there are many ways to be water.

I would like to know all the ways of being water, Ea. How can you explain the molecular structure of water, for example?

How you are made up, you are all beings of light, the little drops of water.

That's us dear, we are like those light beings when you saw God's light of love, you know.

Do you want me to share the experience I had, Ea?

Absolutely, Illia, it is necessary to explain what everything consists of, you know.

Thank you for these channelings with you, dear Ea!

Experience
One day in 1998 I went to psychomotoric physiotherapy, to help my body let go of old tensions from traumas.
A strong feeling comes up, that I do not deserve GOD's love.

I sense I am about six years old and know where this thought/feeling comes from.
When I was a child I went to Sunday school near to where I lived, and the priest made us feel like sinners. I was horrified by this and decided to walk the few kilometres home, and brainwash away this untruth. There I said to myself, of course you don't have to be or do anything special to deserve God's love, it's for everyone!

As I approached where the Sunday school had been, I saw two large hands in the air revealing a golden light.
I saw that this love-light is EVERYTHING that exists. I have always thought that asphalt stops mother earth from breathing, but the asphalt was also created by this love-light!
The air is also created by the love-light, so we breathe in love with every breath we take.

I saw small rainbows in the light, and they smiled at me. I have not been depressed or sad after this experience.

In 2020, I asked my soul who the small rainbows were and he said:

It's us. When we finish our journeys on planets and in realities, we go back and become part of the light of love again.

EA – WATER!

Sitting in oneness with the ocean,
feeling the waves roll in.

Feel how the water drops stroke
and caress the rocks,
the sand and our bodies.

The water droplets eagerly await their turn,
dancing over the rocks and sand.

Like fairies dancing in the sunset,
they sweep ashore and out again, to let the next wave
in to dance on the beach.

The water loves us and is part of us.

Fria
Angel of the air

See you dear Fria
in front of me

with your long flowing hair,

you're floating in the air in front of me
as I sit here.

3-12-21

Fria wants me to channel her dimensions, being and element.

Okay dear Fria, are you ready to share your wisdom with me?

I am, dear.

I am grateful that you are listening to me.

How nice to hear, dear.

It will be exciting to make a book together.

What do you want to tell us, Fria?

Your element is also made up of realities and dimensions, isn't it Fria?

It certainly is, dear.

Which reality do you want to start with, Fria?

I'll start with the layer of air without movement. Stagnant air.

What do you mean by stagnant air, Fria?

I mean air that just lies there, without movement,
Illia.
It's inside your lungs, inside your blood vessels.

Yes, of course, wow.
So air that is not moved by force.

(Had to break, I was interrupted.)

7-12-21
Dear Fria, you started to talk about stagnant air.
Is there anything else you want to tell us about
stagnant air?

Yes, Illia, there are many layers of stagnant air.

Are there?

Yes, dear, and the first layer is of course inside your
bodies. Then it goes outwards, but your skin is also
filled with oxygen.
Your skin breathes, and you've always noticed that,
Illia. Because you don't like to wear too many clothes,
you don't like to wear lotion.

It's because you feel like you're stopping me from being
in your skin.

Oh, how strong that you know it, dear Fria!
I've always felt that we breathe through our skin.

We certainly do, dear.
When we get outside of that, we come out into the
real physical dimension. There air becomes something
completely different, don't you think?

It does Fria. Is it moving air then?

It is, dear, but we're not going there yet.
We're going to stay in the motionless air.

I want to tell you there is much more air in things
than you think there is.
Air is everywhere on earth and inside earth.

Is it, Fria? I didn't know that.

You know that there is air in crystals, air in
mountains, in masses and in clay.

Yes, so that is stagnant air?

That's it, dear.

But what is it about that air, and what else would you like to tell us about the stagnant air?

That air there is magical, Illia.

Is it?

Yes, because it contains so much from history.
The air inside crystals, Illia, contains much that no longer exists, from before time.
It contains the history, Illia, you can read the history in oxygen, oxygen in things.

Wow, how exciting.

Yes, you see, they will read the history in air eventually, you see. Based on the molecules and atoms found in the still air.
Then they will learn a lot about life earlier on earth.

Sounds exciting, but Fria, are you everywhere or just within the earth's aura?

I'm only within the earth's aura, Illia.

Okay, so the element air only exists on earth.

It does, dear.

Of course, they don't have oxygen anywhere else.

No, they don't, there's more ethereal mass elsewhere, Illia.

That's right, I just haven't thought along those lines, Fria.

There is only air on earth. It was created so that you can live with your bodies here, you know.

I would like to tell you a fairy tale, Illia.
The fairy tale about the creation of the air on earth, you see.
About the stagnant air, before movement came into being.

That sounds exciting.
So the earth is like a cell, isn't it?

**It is, dear, and the oxygen exists throughout the cell.
From the membrane.**

All planets have their own essence they breathe in.
And they have their own cell membrane, also within
their own cell membrane.

That's how it is, dear.

This is special to think of.
That we are cells in a body. And whose body is it that
we are all cells in?
So strong, I dare not think about it!
It got me into strange thoughts, Fria.

I can understand that, dear. God is great, you know.

Hey, I'm starting to get it now. I can't think about it,
we are on the topic air now.

(Had an experience in the 90's where I got the idea
that we are all God's thought manifested cells!)

Inside earth before the movement came into being I
was still, Illia.
Without movement in the whole.

Tell me more, Fria, do you want to use my voice or is
it easier for you to speak into my heart?

Much easier, Illia.

Okay, then I'll say your words into the recording of
our conversation.

I'll tell you, there's a lot more to oxygen than you
think.
There are layers of atoms, on different levels in air.

How many atoms and molecules does air consist of?

We won't go into that here, Illia. It's too chemical and
physical.
I will tell you that oxygen is made up of many
components which scientists don't know about.

It's on a different level than physical, and scientists don't see that, Illia.

No, I guess they don't?

There is a level of magic that air can create, you see.

Uh, what?

Air creates all the time dear, you have not known it, that's why you have thought so negatively about air. About pollution and all, but air has its own creative power, you see.

It does, it's so magical.

Air has its own creative power, Illia.
Because it can create exactly what it needs, for the best welfare of earth and itself.

Wow, I feel you creating harmony in the oxygen in my body, Fria. I feel the healing you give me now, very strong.
Oh, dear Fria, I feel you healing all the oxygen in my body.

It is pure love, your oxygen.
In the oxygen of your cells, you are pure love now.

Thank you, Fria, for the magical healing.

There will be more, dear.

9-12-21
Dear Fria, would you like to tell us more about the stagnant air on earth?

I will tell you that it is very magical, the stagnant air inside things.
All history from the origin of earth is there.

Exciting, Fria. Are you ready to go to the next one, or is there more you want to tell us about stagnant air?

There's more there dear, there's a lot more on stagnant air. On a completely different level than the other levels.

Wow, suddenly it stopped blowing, so strange!

We were disturbed, and I'm stopping now because I feel like I can't do it now.

I understand, dear.

27-4-22
It's been a very long time since we last spoke, Fria. I have fled from the channelings with you, Fria.
I was frightened when the storm suddenly disappeared and we were disturbed.

Dear Fria, you wanted to tell me more about stagnant air on other levels of being. So which level of being are they?

There are levels where everything is in unity with a being that exists only in still air.

Yes, but isn't that you, Fria?

**Yes, but me on another level of reality.
A level where we exist alone, without being in connection with anything else.**

What do you mean, I don't quite understand.

It is being in another existence, like being in the present with the all in the All, in the sphere of still air.

It tells me nothing, Fria.

I understand, dear, but I will try to explain in another way.
The being in still air is a substance, a mass of energy and creation.

What does it create?

It creates human desires into reality.

What? Where does the stagnant air exist then?

It exists inside your brains, and there you create desires with this air.

That sounds strange, dear.

I understand, but that air assists you in your thought creation.

How so?

By saving your thoughts forever, dear ones, that's why it's so important to think good, constructive thoughts.

Yes, it is very important!
Wow, our human body is strangely complex.

Yes, it is, dear, much more complex than you can imagine.

Is there anything else you want to tell us about this stagnant air dear?
I found it a bit difficult to understand that your energy is involved in storing our thoughts.
So I have released a lot of your stagnant energy, dear, through my cleansing of old beliefs/convictions?

You certainly have, dear, and through your work over the last four years you have helped me and released many souls from their thought mass.
And we are very grateful for your great work there.

Think of all the people you have managed to
transform into souls.
And all the old thought matter they have released,
during your love's transformation of their egos into
enlightened souls.

Then I think, Fria, where does that thought-energy
air go from there?

Then it goes back to my element, all air.

Does it become stagnant or moving air again?

It is then transformed into moving, free air, free from
its prison in the mass of human thought.

What do you mean by prison?

Thoughts were meant to come and go,
but humans have gotten completely caught up in the
ego's aberrations in their heads.
That's how my air has become trapped in your minds.

Wow, so strong, Fria. Strange but also
understandable.

So how does it feel for you to be a prisoner in people's brains?

It feels locked in, an unnatural state of being for my air.

Do you notice it in any way?

I feel it as frozen energy in my body. As you experience when you lock history in your body, you get stiff muscles and joints.

Do you feel it as discomfort?

Not discomfort, just stagnation and bad breath. Hehe.

You have a sense of humour, dear.

Yes, humour is important, you know.

Yes, lovely with humour. How do you want to proceed now?

Now I want to go to another level of my existence as air.

This level is a much more important level, where we really depend on people for our existence.
I need their attention to thrive and grow.

Grow, are you going to grow?

Yes, everything expands, Illia, on many levels you see.

On what level are you thinking of then, Fria?

I will tell you of a level of my air you don't know exists.

Wow, what level is that?

It is the level of creation in eternity.

Creation in eternity, I do not understand.

It is not so easy to understand, Illia, but I would like to include it in this magical book of yours, dear Illia.

This creating in eternity is about how things come into being in other realities here on earth.

As you have channeled from Razul, there are many realities on earth that humans never experience. These are realities beyond normal human understanding. Because this is about air in other forms of energy.

So there is air on a different level than the air we know? Is that what you mean?

That's it, dear.

This is special to talk about, dear. I feel something happening in my body as I say this and hear your voice in my heart.
What are you doing to me now?

I'm trying to make you experience me in other realities dear Illia.

I'm unable to explain what I feel, but somehow I'm covered with a different kind of air!
Am I explaining myself correctly now, Fria?

You are, but there was a mass of air on another level enveloping your body, dear.

How many levels of air can I manage to experience?

Many, as long as you are with me, and I explain it to you along the way.

I understand, dear, it was a special experience.
Thank you for giving me these experiences, dear.

Is this what I feel in the same way when other and unknown energies enter my aura?
But this energy did not feel threatening in any way.

That's it, dear.

What do you want to tell us now, Fria?

What I want to share with you now is another reality of air that exists on earth. It is air which exists in your being.

You mean the soul in the heart?

No, Illia, your ego-soul, located in the back of your brain and controls your desires, such as survival desires and other types of desires.
It is the air of your ego self, which is in your ego's thoughts and desires.
This is very compressed, heavy air which is seldomly released, like what we talked about earlier coming out of the ones you release, Illia.

Was that the same thing you said earlier that we have creative air in our brains?

No, not quite the same. This is your ego since you took up residence in your first body as angels.
That air is there until the ego becomes enlightened, one with the soul.
Only then will the old survival thought patterns, the old air, be released from the body.
What happens then is that all development happens much faster than before, so it's very important to enlighten the ego, Illia.

The masters have told you in your previous books how important it is to love the ego.

And thank it for keeping you alive by giving you hunger and thirst and protection for the survival of your body.

By giving you feelings similar to an old experience, to prepare you for survival mode.

And this is what the old air is part of, the survival strategy of the ego, because history is stored in the air.

The ego brings memories from the air into your feelings and thoughts, to remind you to be alert as something dangerous might happen.

It is my air which brings the story to the ego that warns you!

Wow, so strong!

So your air is part of our ego's memory bank?

That's right, dear.

Something so strange, but when you explain it, it becomes understandable. But I've never been in these lines of thought before.

No, it's because it's something new, an unknown reality for most people.

Now I want to move on to the air you breathe into your physical bodies.
This is also magical air full of possibilities you haven't heard of before.
The air you breathe also has history you can connect with as it moves inward and down into your body.

Oh, I felt it just now, the consciousness in the air I breathed in. Wow, so surreal and magical at the same time.
What can we absorb from this air?

Oh, I feel you filling me with you, Fria. And I cry because it releases something old in me.
What happened, Fria?

I infused you with lots of love dear, so that old longings for love from when you were a child could pass out forever.

Oh, it was so beautifully powerful and greatly liberating, dear Fria.
Now I feel freer and lighter in my body.
Can everyone ask for such healing from you, Fria?

They can, dear, but first they need to establish
contact as you have done, Illia.
They need to know that I am there for everyone, and
everyone can talk to me as you do, Illia.

So please everyone, talk to the elements. We are
angels like you. It's just that we have chosen to become
an element and you have chosen a physical body in
this unfoldment of life, in physical reality.

It was a very strong experience, Fria. I feel the air I
breathed in with your consciousness continues to work
in my body.

Yes, dear, now I am on my way from the lungs into
your heart and onwards with my consciousness out
into the veins and the thin capillaries in your body.

I feel how the healing spreads outwards and
approaches my little hair capillaries in the skin.
Thank you, Fria, for a magical healing that just goes
on and on in my body!

Yes, now you get my greatest healing dear Illia, as a thank you for your love for my element.

Oh dear, I feel so touched by your love which fills me from the inside and out, Fria.
THANK YOU.

We stop here today, dear. Lie down and feel my love for you, Illia.

I will, dear goddess of the air.

28-4-22
It was a strong healing I received yesterday. Today I feel changed, but I can't explain it.
What happened Fria?

What happened is that I want to help you so much, past the despair of your path, feeling like you're not getting enough done. I burned away your old story of despairing of yourself.

Thank you, Fria, I'm very grateful for that healing.
It touched me deeply yesterday and I slept like a rock.

I feel relaxed and changed today, and do not recognize myself because my mood is totally changed.

I understand, dear, you are different today on many levels.

Before, I had contact with the Divine energy in my heart, but today I feel contact with the Divine in my whole body!

There you have it, dear.

It was a strong healing you gave me, Fria.

You needed it, you see. I cleared out a lot of stagnant air from your brain and your body, dear.

That's good to hear, dear.
Which dimension/reality of air do you want to talk about today, Fria?

I want to tell you about reality in matter.

What matter do you want to tell us about?

Matter as a part of the whole of air.

As the matter of air, is that what you mean?

That's it, dear.

So, what do you want to tell me about it?

I want to say that matter air is an energy of its own.

Do you mean specifically the air, not oxygen, but air in general?

Air in general, Illia, air in general also has a matter on a different level than the physical oxygen.

Which level is it, Fria?

There is a level of creation in the invisible.

So, how do you create in the invisible?
It doesn't have anything to do with our physical dimension, does it?

It certainly does, Illia, because you create so much with your mind that you have no idea you're doing.

Yes, that is true.

So, it's very important to know that thoughts also create in the invisible.

I don't quite understand this.

When you go and think and let your thoughts take over and let them run in unison in your head and listen to them, then you create the realities you think of in other places. In other dimensions and realities.

Do we?

Yes, you are some great creators and need to know this.

Wow, now I realize how important it is to stop listening to our heads.

Very important, Illia, we can't say it often enough how important it is to stop and listen to the head.

It's a treasure trove to be used, but to listen to, it's just history repeating itself, over and over again.

That's really bad. Can you give us an exercise, Fria, which can make it easier for people to stop listening to their heads?

I can do that.
I would like to share a nice exercise to make it easier to stop following your head instead of your heart.

Exercise: "Changing your old beliefs"

Sit with your eyes closed.
Bring out a thought you're not happy with about yourself, people, or life.
Whatever it is.

Yes, the feeling that life is difficult comes to mind.

What happens my dear, when you think the thought that life is difficult, then you create that thought into reality. On another level, another dimension.
The way not to create the thought which comes, is to delete the thought as soon as it arrives.

To erase the thought, you do by saying:
But this is not mine, goodbye, goodbye.

Oh God, I felt it releasing, that life is hard.

You see, Illia, we have told you many times, both your
souls and we know that the simple way is the best!
Magic is very, very simple, dear.

The same as I did when I was sitting on the couch and
felt a sense of depression enter my aura.
I thought: do I have any reason to be depressed now?
I'm not starving and I'm not cold and have everything
I need.
Then I said "bye!". The depressive thought bothered
me for three days, but it has never since returned!

You can do the same with your thoughts, Illia.

Fantastic, Fria, such a great and wonderful message.
It is very important. A magical experience, dear.
Then it is very important to listen without judging
your brain.

Not really, Illia, it can be done much easier. Every
time a thought about yourself, humanity, or life comes
up, find out if it's something you want to believe in
here and now.
And if it's not, then say: this is not my thought
anymore, so goodbye!

Wow, my whole body shakes just saying that, Fria.

It's magic on a high level, Illia. There are very few who
believe it can be so easy.
It really is that easy, Illia.

I can feel it, a lot happened in my body.
I'm going to sit and work with all my thoughts now.

Remember, Illia, you can't take too much at once, six
thoughts per day is enough.

Thank you, I really liked that exercise, Fria.
How exciting. We create what we think. It's maybe
not visible in our reality, but in other dimensions and
realities not visible to humans.

That's how it is, Illia.

How can we remove what has already been thought
and created?

It is impossible, dear, for it is already created.

So when we think of war, we create war?

You certainly do, Illia.

Oh, God, that's terrible.

**Yes, you must be very careful what you use your mind
for, dear ones.
By all means, you need to remember you are very
great creators. Remember you all are angels, creating
with everything; words, thoughts and deeds. Creating
realities in other dimensions and realities.**

So strong. Would you like to say something more,
Fria?

**We'll wait until later, Illia, because you were deeply
shaken.**

Yes, I feel transformed, very strongly.

6-4-22

Full moon

Sorry Fria, but I have been busy finishing the book "Planets and realities".

You told me you wanted to channel more, and I feel ready now that I have submitted "Planets and realities" to the publisher.

You told me last time about something that happens when I connect with you. What happens then, Fria?

What happens, Illia, is that you heal and send love to all air on earth and inside all human bodies, Illia.

Oh, it's so big that I don't know if I can understand how powerful this is.

I understand, dear, but you are the greatest master on earth right now, you know.
Even if you look down on yourself, you are the greatest master on earth, Illia.

I find it hard to understand that what I do is so important.

It is much more important than you think, dear. You are healing the earth with your love and filling that love into all air on the whole earth and everything that breathes air, including humans.

You told me Fria last time, that we can connect to the air we breathe and draw wisdom from that air. We can do it by feeling that air. Can we also ask for an answer to something specific?

You can, dear ones, you can ask for anything, it's all stored in the air.
All history that has been on earth is stored in the air, which you can bring down when you breathe in.
Just ask for the wisdom you want, and I will give it to you in the air you breathe.

Are we able to receive it freely?
Or do we receive it even if we are not awake enough to receive it?

You will receive what you have asked for, but you may not perceive it clearly.
It will be stored in your history, as a memory.

How wonderful! How do you want us to focus on the air we breathe in, Fria?

I want you to focus on breathing in knowledge. The total knowledge of planet earth and its history. Everything is in our air, you see, everything is in the air around the earth which you breathe in every day. You can connect to and receive wisdom from it.

What is the easiest way to receive this wisdom, dear? Should we hear it as thoughts, feelings, or images?

It can be all three, it depends on how open you are on the different levels.
Everyone has different abilities; some hear very well, others see, and some get images.
You receive what you are able to receive, and your body stores what you have asked for.

Sounds magical, Fria. Is there anything else you want to tell us about the air we breathe?

Yes, it's magical air, Illia. A magical air that contains
so much life force that humans don't think of, that
the air contains life force.
And there is creative power in the air, you are
breathing in creative power.

Wow, how exciting. So how can we use the air to
create with, Fria?

You can create your life from memories which are in
the air, but also that you ventilate your brain with the
new air you breathe in, as you have asked for.
Maybe you will experience more love with the air you
breathe. Then it will wash your brain and bring in
more loving thoughts instead of old dirt.

Is it really possible, Fria?

It is, Illia, you know it's much easier than you think.
It's consciousness that controls everything dear,
consciousness of what you choose.

Thank you very much. Is there anything else you want
to tell us, or are you done with your element, Fria?

I am, that's the last thing I wanted to tell you, dear.

Thank you, dear Fria!

Arakto

Angel of fire

Sitting in the forest, thinking of the book I'm working
on at the moment, "Angels of the Elements", and the
last element is the element of Fire.
Who is the angel of fire, Seraphim?

Suddenly I see a big angel in front of me!

"My name is Arakto!"

He says with a powerful voice in my heart, so strong
that my whole body jumps from the healing I get
when I am in his energy field.

When I arrive in La Gomera, Spain, there will be
another meeting with Arakto, the angel of fire.
I have been struggling to channel the last few months,
getting disturbed.
Now I am ready for a new meeting with Arakto!

23-1-2023

Today is a new moon and I start talking to Arakto.
He tells me that he controls our hara chakra, he
creates the power, the fire in us.
The life force is part of Arakto's element in us
humans.
Looking forward to the next conversation with
Arakto.

4-2-23

Sitting in the forest listening to the beautiful bird
song and I am ready to channel Arakto.

Dear Arakto, what would you like to tell me about
your element of fire?
I have never read about fire as an element, and only
think of it as lava and volcanoes.

**I want to tell you that the element of fire is so much
more than you think it is.**

You told me your element is connected to our hara chakra, that you represent the fire and creativity in the hara chakra.

I do.

Do tell, Arakto.

I am a great angel, and you have seen it, Illia.

I have, Arakto, I also feel you in my body as you use my voice.

I am so grateful to you for channeling my wisdom, dear Illia.

I am very grateful that you want to talk to me, Arakto.

Remember, we have been waiting for contact with humanity for thousands of years, thousands of lives. It has been too primitive here to make it happen in the past.

Now I will tell you how my element works.

Thank you, Arakto.

I live inside the earth.

The element of fire on earth is best known from lava.
It spurts fire, red-hot rock from the earth's interior.

That's not the most important thing about my
element, dear.

Is it not?

My element, fire, is the fire in people.
The fire, the life force in people is really my element.
Also in the animals and insects.
In a way, I am the driving force in people, in their
physical bodies.

I've never heard of this before, Arakto.

That's why your book is so important, my dear.
When you channel us elements, you get to know us in
the right way.

Very grateful for that, Arakto.

I will tell you that it is a very exciting element, you
see.
My element belongs to the law of action on the
magical level.
I live in the reality of magic all the time, Illia.

How do you create fire with magic?

I create with the element of fire, your events.

What kind of events, Arakto?

Events in life. I am the driving force behind the events.

Fria has stored your thoughts in the air in your
brains, I am the one who brings them out.
I am the driving force in your body.

Wow!
You have many levels of existence, don't you?

I have, dear.

You're on one level inside the human body?

That's the beauty of it.
Exciting, isn't it, Illia?

Yes, very exciting. This is new wisdom which I've never heard before.

No, there are very few people who know this, Illia.

It shakes my body from the healing I get when you use my voice.

You get strong healing from me, you need it now, you see, on a level you have never received healing before, you know.

I feel it, it's on a completely different level. I can feel it in my muscles.

I am the driving force that makes the muscles work, dear. That drives you forward, to action.
Also the creation of old untruths you have stored in your brain with Fria, in the air in your brain.

That was powerful to hear. Is there anything else you want to tell us about the human body?

No, we're done on that level now. We're going to move on to the level of thought.

Are you in our thoughts too, Arakto?

I am also the driving force of thoughts, not just the creation of thoughts. I also drive thoughts from Fria's air in the brain into action.

So you are the force of action of all living things?

I am, my dear.

Oh, it's so powerful.
I feel like I've been missing you inside me all my life, dear.

I know, but it's happening now, you see.

My body shakes from healing and crying, so I must stop now.

5-2-23

Sitting in the forest again and looking forward to talking to Arakto.

Do you want to talk about thoughts, about your presence in our minds?

Yes dear, I am present in your thoughts and drive them to creation.

I create what you have thought. I am the driving force, creating what you have thought.

Is it you who create it?

It's created by what we believe in, isn't it?

Your beliefs create thoughts, but I am the one who drives them into reality, who manifests them physically, dear.

Wow, that's powerful. Is there anything else you want to tell us about thoughts and your presence in the mind, Arakto?

I would like to share an experience with you, Illia, where you can choose to join in, or just listen to what I tell you.

How can I join, Arakto?

We can make it happen in your body, dear.

Oh wow, okay! What do you want me to do, Arakto?

Close your eyes and take it easy, get comfortable and breathe deeply into your stomach.
Now create a thought you want to remove, Illia.

Yes, that I am different, perhaps?

That thought is almost gone for you, you've already removed many in different variations.

Yes, I have, dear.

I want you to take that thought and look up into the pituitary gland/crown chakra and place it with the Christ light.

Pull the light up and present the belief that you are not valuable.
Then I create a change while you focus in the middle of your head.

I don't believe that anymore, I choose to believe that I am very valuable.

Then I manifest it, dear.

Oh, my whole body is shaking.
A nice exercise to share in the book.

It's very important, Illia, tell them how important it is to be aware, so they do not let other thoughts in.

Okay, suddenly the feeling that I am valuable comes, Arakto. Thank you very much, Arakto.
It happened right away, the feeling of being valuable came into my body right away.

Yes, I'm a magician, you know.

Yes, I understand that now.

The others can't do that exercise without help from you, Arakto, can they?

No, I must be involved, for it is I who remove the old untruth and replace it with a new one.
New creation in your reality, my dear.

I would never have thought that the element of fire could be inside our bodies in the way you tell, Arakto. It surprises me very much.

I know dear, there are very few who have the knowledge you are getting now, you see.
So this book is very important, Illia.
Very important it is, so people will know who they really are.

Then I think this channeling today will also be included in the book "Who are we?" which will come later?

I definitely think so, Illia.

Then I'll do it.
Thank you very much, dear.

Is there anything else you'd like to tell me about the
thought level?

I'm done with your body now, dear. Let's get back to
nature.

It shakes all over me when you use my voice and
channel, dear. I get tired after a few minutes.
Is there anything else you want to tell me today?

We'll continue tomorrow.

Exercise: Connect with the divine spark of love in your
heart.
Channeled to me 25th of December 2018.

Close your eyes, breathe deeply into your belly, place
your left hand on your heart and feel the energy from
your hand into your heart. Look inwards into your
heart.
There you will see the divine light.
It may be a small star, or a flame.
Bring the light down into your belly and let it rest
there for a while. Then bring it up to your head. Leave
it there for a while, bring it down to your left

shoulder, then over to your right shoulder, into your right arm, leave it there for a while. Then go up and over to the left shoulder and go up and down the left arm. Now bring the light back to the heart again. Focus on the heart, then send it slightly backwards and guide the light backwards into the spine.
Send it up and down the spine, and then back to the heart.

It's a great exercise which can be used as often as possible to cleanse the body of pain and old history. The more often you do it, the more healing you will get, and the light gets bigger and bigger.

6-2-23
Dear Arakto, yesterday you told us how you work with your fire in our minds.
You said you were done talking about the body and were going over to nature.
So, what do you want to tell us about nature, Arakto?

I am in nature's energy creation, Illia.

What do you mean, you're the one who makes things grow?

I am part of the energy which creates growth. The energy of fire helps to create growth and change in nature on many levels.

What level do you want to start with, Arakto?

I want to start with the etheric level, outside the human body, in the aura of the earth.

I will talk about how I manifest in your air, which you breathe.
There is also creation with molecules when you breathe in.
As you saw when you saw the Divine Love Light and as you breathe in the Love Light. I am part of the love light on earth.
I am the manifested part of that love light on earth and the fire element, Illia.

I haven't thought about it because one thinks all goes by itself. I know it's more complex, but I don't think in those terms.

So you are there in the air we breathe and create
change in our air too, Arakto?

**I'm helping to create the energy of love, so that you
can breathe in the energy of love.
Because as you know, Illia, everything is love.**

I have been shown it and been in it as divine beings
have given me the experience that everything is
created by the light/energy of love.
That was in 1998, and I have not been depressed a
day since.
Except when I despair over my own limitations, stuck
in old habits.
Good to see that we breathe in the energy of love
with every breath we take, very magical.
So what are you in that love air, Arakto?

**I am the driving force that carries it into your
bloodstream from your lungs, Illia.**

So you carry the love light from the lungs into the
bloodstream along with oxygen?

I do, my dear.

Is there anything else you want to tell me about the air on earth?

No, that's all for now. Now I'll move on to the more physical level of the earth.

Are you thinking about plants and animals?

The same applies to animals as it does to you, dear ones, I work in the same way as I do for humans. But there it's the reflex and intuition I help to create into action. They have no thoughts, animals don't think, they act on reflexes.
And that's where I help them and make it easier for them to reflect on and live their lives in their own best interests, along with the ego in their brains.

So the animals and insects also have an ego?

Yes, they need it for survival, you know, otherwise everything is just love and they wouldn't survive a day on earth, dear. At least not more than 2-3 days.

Of course! So plant life, what do you do in plant life?

I help with the growth of plants, dear.

I help with the photosynthesis from light to oxygen to nutrients in the plant.

I am the driving force in plants.

So strong, I never thought fire could be part of the plant kingdom, too!

I am in everything, just as Fria and Ea are in everything, so am I in everything, Illia.

I'm beginning to understand that now, Arakto, it's very powerful to know.

Is there another level in the plant kingdom where you work?

No, that's what I do in the plant kingdom.

What about the mineral kingdom, dear?

I get to that now, dear.

I am also in the mineral kingdom in creation, and there we are back to lava, Illia. Then I am inside the earth, where I help to send lava upwards with the power of fire to make lave splash out of the earth.

So you're not inside rocks, then?

My memory is in crystals, Illia.

So the element of fire is stored in crystals?

Absolutely dear, I am stored in the history of crystals, there is my being and my creation stored.

So that's why we can put higher energy into stones? Because you create it in your energy in crystals/stones?

That's how it is, dear.

As you manifest our thoughts into creation, it is also in minerals in the creation there?

Absolutely dear. But it is on a much deeper level in the earth than where lava comes up.

Lava comes from within the earth, with liquid magma coming up. And so I create crystals all along the way with my fire, my creative power.

Do you also work inside the earth?

Inside the earth I create oscillations with my fire, my creative power.
Both in the elf realm, the angelic realm, and the troll realm.
On the same level as you, but in another reality, another level of consciousness.

So you work on all levels in beings of consciousnesses?

I do, dear.

Is there anything else you wish to tell us about your element, Arakto?

You're done with my element now, Illia.

Have you told me everything?

I have, dear.

Thank you, dear, I can feel you healing me all over my body.
Goodbye for now.

There will never be goodbye with us elements, Illia, you are one with us all the time, you see. After you contacted us, we became one on a very specific level. On the angelic level we are one all the time my dear sister.

Dear Arakto, thank you so much for helping me with my thoughts yesterday. Today I actually feel valuable, I have only done so for a moment one time, after an assignment I received from Seraphim on the airplane where I sent love to the clouds.
Seraphim told me that then it rains love to earth. The water in our bodies also receives love because water has memory.
It is very magical.
I will be contacting you for more help with old untruths.

Please do.

Farewell for now, dear angel of fire Arakto.

Thank you, father and mother God, the guiding principle of the love that fills me and everything else that IS!

I asked my masters when I started channeling in 2018, what was the small rainbows?

It is us angels when we are done traveling the universes!

I feel so honoured to have the great trust from the elements so that they choose me to channel their wisdom on this beautiful, physical planet.

We, all four elements on earth, would like to wish you all to connect with us.
That way we can assist you in your lives.

And remember, we are eagerly awaiting your contact and will be delighted to have conversations with you.

When you contact us, remember it is in your heart
that the voice comes, and only there can you hear our
wisdom.

Thank you God, thank you Seraphim and thank you
Osiris.
It's so powerful to be all four of us together.

The channeled books

"Bullied into Love" are conversations with masters from the various indigenous peoples and from other realities and planets.

"Osiris book 1", is about the Egyptian God Osiris from Sirius.
He is my life mission soul who sends me on missions around the world.
There, Osiris creates lines that hold the earth in its oval journey in the universe.

"1. with the soul", in that book, where you follow my journey towards oneness with my soul/higher self archangel Seraphim, guardian angel of the Muslims, just as Christianity has the archangel Michael as its guardian angel.

"Planets and realities", here Seraphim channels his wisdom, and we have conversations and journeys in the universes.

Feel free to contact me by email if you have any questions.
E-mail: aandevokter@gmail.com

I would love to share the books that have lifted me into new paths of consciousness!

"The Life and Teachings of the Eastern Of the far east" 1-3
Baird T. Spalding

Book 1 is free to read in English.
You can also find book 1 on youtube.com.
There are 2 readers, and the women are more emotional when reading.

"Journey into nature"
"Journey into oneness"
Michael J. Roads

"Ramtha"
J. Z. Knight